Contents

A wasteful world

I magine what would happen if nobody took your rubbish away. If day after day, week after week, your rubbish piled up in your house and garden.

Pretty soon you would be wading through plastic bottles and paper bags and rotting food. It would look terrible and the smell would be worse. If we don't control the amount of waste we throw away, this situation might actually happen!

We live in a very wasteful world. Almost everything we do creates waste. Everything we buy, everything we eat, everything we use all produces waste that has to be disposed of in some way.

As the population of the world grows, the amount of rubbish produced increases too. The problem is not just that our society produces more waste today than ever before, but it is also doing it at a greater rate. Today we produce three times as much waste as we did in the 1960s.

⊙ A strike by refuse collectors in Leeds, England in October 2009 shows what our streets look like after just a few weeks with no collections.

The large volumes of rubbish we make, creates not just a disposal problem, but is also a huge waste of **natural resources**. Unless things can be reused or **recycled**, everything we throw away has to be produced again out of new materials. More trees have to be cut down to make paper; more oil has to be refined to make plastic. Prevention of waste is a better solution than even the best way of disposing of it.

Disposal of waste has become critical throughout the world. Where does the waste come from? How do we get rid of it? How can we reduce the amount of it? Finding ways to deal with the waste we produce is one of the major problems facing the world today.

A large proportion of our rubbish is disposed of in **landfill** sites. But landfill is an ugly, polluting and environmentally unfriendly way to dispose of waste.

Domestic waste

Many people buy a daily newspaper, drink cola from an aluminium can or coffee from a polystyrene cup. All these things are used once and then thrown away.

Inside the bin

If we look at the waste an average household produces, you will see that the largest amount comes from leftover food and garden waste. After this, paper and card are the biggest contributors. Over half of this comes from newspapers and magazines. Much of our rubbish is plastic (packaging and bottles) and glass (bottles and jars) which makes up nearly a quarter of our waste.

⊙ This piechart shows the proportions of the types of waste produced in an average household.

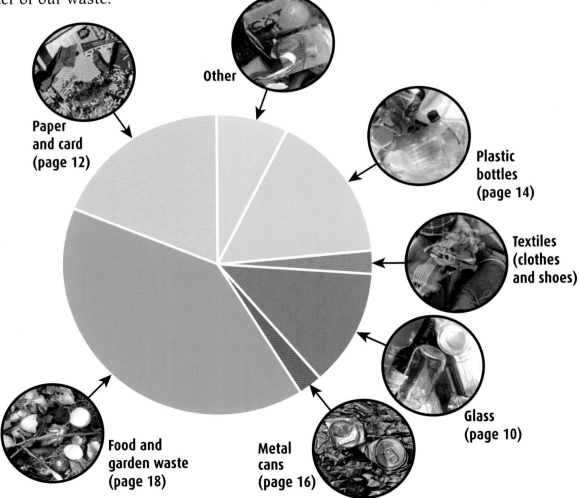

Other

Paper and card (page 12)

Plastic bottles (page 14)

Textiles (clothes and shoes)

Glass (page 10)

Food and garden waste (page 18)

Metal cans (page 16)

So where does it all go?

Most houses bag up their rubbish in special refuse sacks or bins and it is collected by a refuse truck. Some waste products such as paper, glass, plastic, metal and garden waste can be recycled and these are collected separately.

In most countries the majority of un-recyclable waste is sent to landfill. This means it is buried in the ground. Some is **incinerated**, which means it is burned. Dealing with our rubbish in this way is not a very good solution. When we bury or burn rubbish we are polluting the land and **atmosphere**. Most landfill sites are nearly full and we are running out of land for new sites.

⊙ The average household in the UK produces more then a tonne of waste every year. This adds up to a total of 31 million tonnes per year, equivalent to the weight of three and a half million double-decker buses.

Every nation needs to find ways of reducing the amount of waste they produce, recycling more of it and disposing of what is left over more carefully.

▶ In most residential areas, household waste is picked up and taken away by refuse collectors. Most of it is disposed of in landfill sites or incinerated.

Reduce, reuse, recycle

To help solve the waste problem we need to *reduce* the amount of rubbish we create, *reuse* as much of our rubbish as possible and *recycle* more of it.

The three Rs

There are three main reasons to reduce, reuse and recycle.

- It saves natural resources. For example, if we reduce the amount of paper we use, we will cut down fewer trees.
- It stops pollution and reduces landfill.
- It saves money. Recycling is usually cheaper than making new things because it uses fewer resources and less energy.

How can you help?

REDUCE: Most countries have a mailing preference service which will remove your name and address from mailing lists reducing the amount of junk mail you receive (right).

REUSE: Give old books and toys to playgroups, hospitals or charity shops.

RECYCLE: Turn food waste from your kitchen into compost for your garden.

⊕ Many products we buy are wrapped in unnecessary layers of packaging. If manufacturers used less packaging it would reduce the amount of waste in our bins by a huge amount.

Waste disposal by country

How countries dispose of their waste often depends on their size. Large countries have a lot of space to bury their waste so Canada and the USA dispose of more than half their waste in this way. Small countries do not have large areas of land available for landfill and so incinerate or recycle more of their rubbish. For example, both Japan and Denmark send over half their waste for incineration while Switzerland recycles a massive 76 per cent of its waste.

HOTSPOT:

Disposable nappies

One of the worst creators of waste today is the disposable nappy (below). Their manufacture uses huge amounts of paper, plastic, power and water. As a single item they take up the largest proportion of a landfill's volume. They also take hundreds of years to **biodegrade**. If more parents used cloth nappies it would greatly reduce landfill and help save natural resources.

Recycling glass

Glass is a material that is particularly suitable for recycling. It can be melted down and used over and over again, without losing its quality or strength.

The recycling process

Waste glass is collected in bottle banks or by kerbside collection. The glass is taken to a recycling plant where it is sorted into different colours, cleaned and crushed. The crushed glass is called cullet and this is melted down and used in the production of new bottles or jars.

⊙ Piles of crushed glass at a recycling plant. The UK glass industry recycled over 1.6 million tonnes of glass in 2008, saving enough energy to launch 20 space shuttle missions!

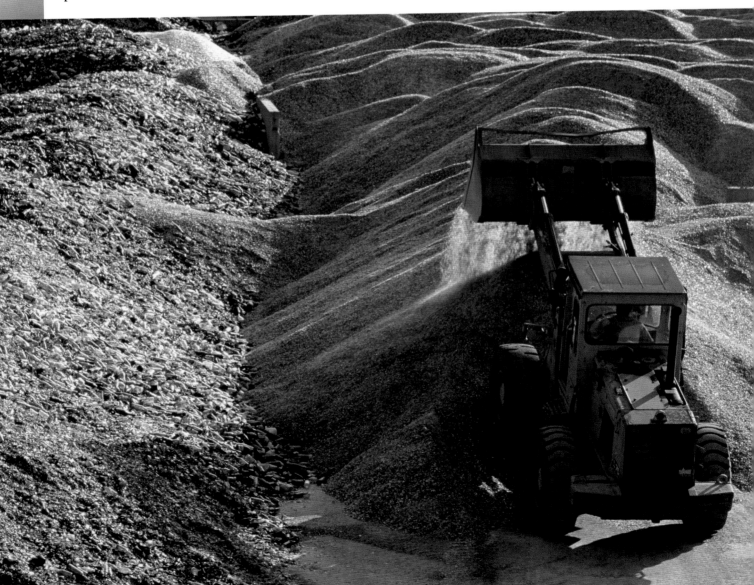

Environmentally friendly

Materials such as sand, limestone and soda are used when making new glass. Recycling glass allows natural resources to be conserved. Energy can also be saved – resulting in a reduction in pollution too. When new glass is made the **furnace** has to be heated to a very high temperature, using huge amounts of energy. But when glass is recycled the temperature of the furnace can be cooler, saving energy and reducing pollution.

⊙ These bottles are being made of recycled glass. The energy saved from recycling one glass bottle can run a 100-watt light bulb for 4 hours.

Big business

In many countries glass, recycling has become a large and profitable business. In the USA glass recycling employs over 30,000 workers in 76 plants. A typical US glass processing plant can recycle up to 20 tonnes of glass per hour and nearly 13 million glass jars and bottles are recycled every day. It is thought that about 37 per cent of the USA's glass bottles and jars are now recycled.

How can you help?

As well as recycling glass bottles and jars, think of other ways to use them. Fill them with homemade jam or chutney or decorate them and use them as flower vases or pencil pots.

Recycling paper

Disposing of paper is a big problem because we use such large amounts of it. Every day we read from it, write on it and buy products wrapped in it. Most of this is thrown away after one use. An average household throws away 13,000 separate pieces of paper each year, made up mostly of packaging and junk mail.

How can you help?

As well as recycling paper, try to reduce the amount you use and reuse more. Use both sides of a piece of paper, reuse wrapping paper, cut up old greetings cards to make new ones or gift tags.

Paper problems

Paper production accounts for about 35 per cent of all trees that are cut down and is responsible for more than 40 per cent of landfill waste. Paper is biodegradable. An unfortunate side-effect of this is that it produces methane, a **greenhouse gas** as it **decomposes**. This may contribute to **global warming**. If more waste paper was recycled it would save trees and help protect the atmosphere.

Recycled paper

Each tonne of recycled paper can save:
17 trees
1,438 litres of oil
three cubic metres of landfill space
4,000 kilowatts of energy
and 30,000 litres of water.

Processing waste paper

Waste paper is collected in paper banks or at the kerbside and taken to a paper mill where it is sorted, graded and mixed with water to form a pulp. The pulp is cleaned and then it is ready to be made into new paper products. Producing recycled paper uses much less energy and water than making new paper from wood. Every tonne of recycled paper can save enough electricity to run a 3-bedroom house for one year.

Quality	Use
This table shows the products recycled paper can be made into. What it is used for depends on the quality of the recycled paper.	
High	Writing paper
Medium	Newspaper, wrapping paper, toilet paper
Low	Cardboard, packaging

HOTSPOT:

European paper champions

Paper is the most recycled product in Europe, and Europe is the global champion in paper recycling with a rate of 64.5 per cent. They hope to increase this to 66 per cent by 2010.

⊙ In California, USA, the law requires that 50 per cent of the paper used in producing newspapers should be recycled paper.

Plastic

Today we use 20 times more plastic than we did 50 years ago. This increase means we have even more to get rid of, and disposing of it is not easy.

The problem with plastic

At present, 8 out of 10 plastic bottles go into landfill. Plastic doesn't rot away. A plastic bottle could take 1,000 years before it even begins to decompose! However, if plastic is burned in an incinerator it emits **poisonous** gases that can pollute the atmosphere. Another problem with plastic is that it is made from oil, a natural resource that is running out. The best solution for getting rid of plastic is to recycle it. That way we can stop wasting a precious natural resource and help the environment.

⊙ These children are visiting a **materials recovery facility** to see how plastic is recycled.

Recycling plastic

One of the problems with recycling plastic is that it is expensive to collect because it takes up a lot of space. That is why when you put your plastic bottles into recycling boxes, you should squash the air out of them. At the recycling centre, plastics are sorted into different types and colours before being shredded into chips and washed. The plastic chips are sent to a plastics factory where they are melted down and used to make new items. Did you know a new fleece top can be made from recycling 25 plastic bottles?

Reducing packaging

Many food products are wrapped in several layers of unnecessary plastic packaging that is not recyclable. Manufacturers, retailers and members of the public need to work together to reduce this wasteful use of plastic. In the UK, 'green' campaigners are calling for all food packaging to be made recyclable by 2013.

How can you help?

The best solution for the plastic problem is to try not to use it at all. Take reusable bags shopping instead of using plastic ones. In the UK, the number of plastic bags handed out has been reduced by half since 2006.

⊙ Recycled plastic can be made into many unusual things. This floating boat jetty is composed of tough, interlocking blocks made of recycled plastic.

Metals

Metals are widely used throughout the world to make items ranging from space rockets to drinks cans. They are found underground as **mineral ores**. These natural resources are limited, so we should conserve them by recycling as much metal as possible.

Recycling metals

The metals that are most easily recycled are aluminium and steel. We use them in many forms of food packaging, from drinks cans to yoghurt pot tops. Before it can be recycled, metal is sorted into steel and aluminium at a waste processing plant. The metals are then sent to a **smelting** works where they are melted down at a very high temperature. Recycled metal products include paper clips, scissors, office furniture, ladders, food and drinks cans, nails and screws.

⊙ In one year in the USA, the recycling of steel saves enough energy to heat and light 18 million homes!

Useful aluminium

Aluminium is one of the most successfully recycled substances. This is lucky since we use over 80 billion aluminium drinks cans every year! Recycling aluminium saves 95 per cent of the energy needed to produce new aluminum from **raw materials**, and there is no limit to the amount of times aluminium can be recycled. The energy saved from recycling one tonne of aluminium is equal to the amount of electricity the average home uses over 10 years.

How can you help?

Reuse metal coat hangers by taking them to your local dry cleaners. Many dry cleaners are trying to keep costs down by reusing coat hangers rather than buying new ones.

It is not possible to reuse drinks cans, so it is important to collect them for recycling.

Biodegradable waste

About one third of waste from households is biodegradable – that means it is capable of rotting away naturally. Biodegradable waste can include grass clippings, fruit and vegetable peelings and other food waste. It also includes both human and animal waste. Biodegradable waste is also produced in large quantities by restaurants, businesses and factories.

Landfill problems

You might think that waste that rots away would be suitable to dispose of in the ground as landfill. But actually this is not a good method of disposal. When biodegradable materials break down they produce methane, a greenhouse gas. About

⊙ We waste a shocking amount of food each year. Each year people in the UK throw away 1.6 billion apples, 484 billion unopened yoghurts and 2.6 billion slices of bread.

one quarter of the UK's methane emissions comes from landfill sites. This is about 2 per cent of the UK's total greenhouse gas emissions. To reduce this amount, biodegradable waste needs to be reused and recycled.

Recycling options

On a small scale, biodegradable waste can be collected in a **compost** bin. The waste is broken down by bacteria (tiny organisms) and eventually forms compost that can be used like **fertiliser** in the garden. However many people live in towns or cities and don't have gardens to collect compost in. In some urban areas, waste is now collected from households and taken to a facility that has a **biodigester**. The biodigester processes the waste and captures the methane that is given off. This can be used for heating or cooking or to generate electricity. The solid waste that is left over is made into fertilisers.

HOTSPOT:
Ludlow biodigester

The residents of Ludlow in the UK have a special waste food collection each week. The food is collected from blue bins (above) and is taken to a nearby biodigester where it is turned into compost, liquid fertiliser and methane. Over 700 tonnes of food waste is recycled in this way each year.

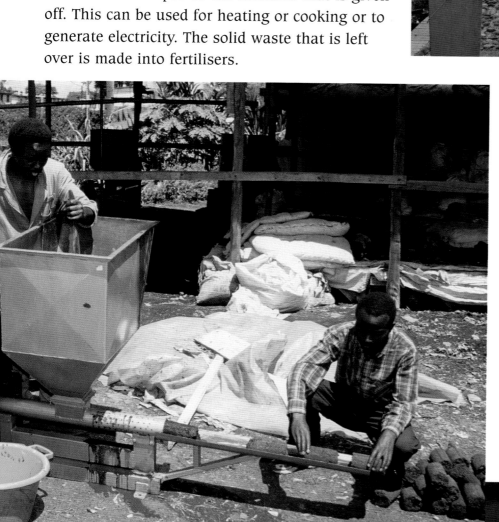

◀ Small communities in **developing countries** often run their own biodigesters on animal manure. These men are making 'logs' from the solid matter left over from their biodigester, which can be used as fuel for cooking and heating.

Landfill and incineration

So what happens to waste that cannot be reused or recycled? It either ends up in landfill or is burnt in an incinerator. Neither of these options is ideal, but there will always be some rubbish that cannot be disposed of in any other way. It is important therefore that both methods are carried out in a way that is least harmful to the environment.

Landfill design

Dumping millions of tonnes of rubbish needs a lot of space. This has often been found in old quarries or mining works. In the past, landfills have created many environmental problems. Rats and pests, seeping liquid pollution, greenhouse gases and litter blowing about are all unwanted side effects of landfill. Now however, landfills are designed much more carefully and managed much better. Once landfill areas are full, they can be covered up and re-landscaped to make parks or other types of recreational area.

▶ This diagram shows how a modern landfill site is constructed and managed.

Each day's rubbish is covered with a layer of soil.

The site has a clay base and is lined with heavy plastic. This prevents any pollution contaminating the water in the ground and soil.

Pipes collect rainwater and any liquid waste.

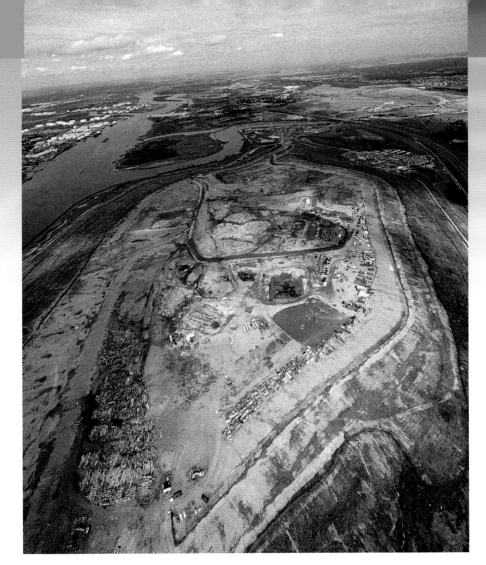

The Fresh Kills landfill site in New York City is so large it can be seen from outer space! Covering 8.9 square km, it will shortly be closed and there are plans to develop the area into a city park and wetland area.

Incineration

Incineration is common in countries like Japan where land is more scarce. About three quarters of Japan's waste is burned in incinerators. This burning of waste is used to recover energy (in the form of steam) for heating and for generating electricity, but it also emits a high concentration of polluting gases which have to be treated before being released into the atmosphere.

Construction industry waste

One of the largest producers of waste is the construction industry. Much of this is packaging. Construction companies are now working with manufacturers to reduce the amount of packaging used. The construction industry aims to achieve a 50 per cent cut in material waste going to landfill by the year 2012.

HOTSPOT:

Too much packaging!

Figures show that in a year, one company supplied 46 kilometres of kitchen worktop, which was wrapped in 90 kilometres of packaging! The company intends to train staff to handle products more carefully so they can reduce the amount of packaging they use.

Dangerous waste

Most of our rubbish may be ugly to look at and can take up a lot of space, but it is not actually dangerous. Some types of waste however are unsafe and more difficult to dispose of.

Electrical items

Every year people buy new televisions, computers or mobile phones. We change batteries and light bulbs without thinking about what they are made of. Many contain poisonous chemicals such as mercury or cadmium or polluting gases. These items need to be taken to specialised centres where they can be dismantled and the **hazardous** substances removed and disposed of properly.

How can you help?

Recycle your mobile phone. Some companies will pay for your old phone. Over 90 per cent of the materials in mobile phones can be recycled and used to make new products.

⊕ Mobile phones contain cadmium, a poisonous metal. They are a hazard if discarded, but can be successfully recycled. Only 10 per cent of mobiles are recycled in the USA each year.

Hospital waste

Hospitals generate many types of contaminated waste. Linen needs to be cleaned and dressings disposed of properly. Waste that is not properly treated can cause infections and dangerous diseases to spread.

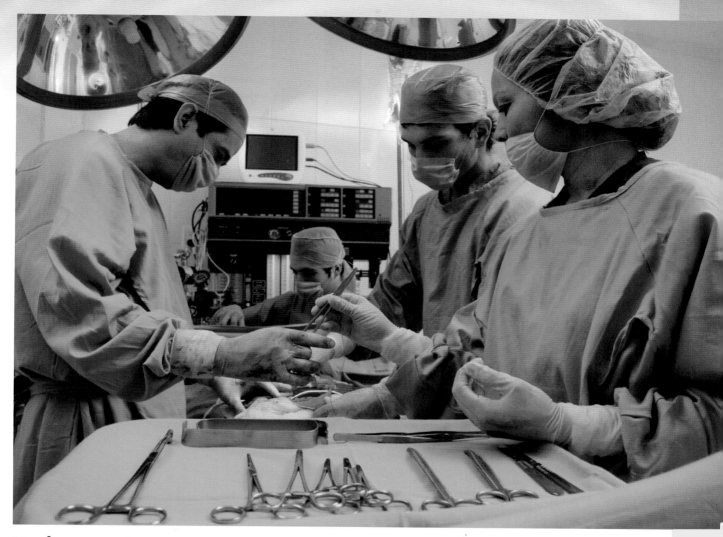

Nuclear waste

Nuclear power stations use **radioactive** materials to generate electricity. This process produces highly dangerous radioactive waste which will be buried in strong chambers deep underground for thousands of years. Although this waste is well contained, many people worry about the possibility of leakage if these areas were struck by earthquakes.

⊙ Surgical instruments can be sterilised at high temperatures and then used again, but needles, scalpels and syringes must be incinerated.

Industrial waste

As well as the waste we produce in our own households, a whole lot more is created by companies that manufacture products. Factories, mills and mines all create waste and each type of industry has its own waste disposal problems.

Thermal pollution

Many industries, especially power stations, use water as a **coolant**. The water is used and returned to rivers, lakes or sea at a higher temperature. This affects the **ecosystem** and fish and other animals can be killed by this 'thermal shock'. However, most industries try to prevent this by installing cooling towers or ponds which transfer the heat to the atmosphere through **evaporation**.

⊙ Fish and other wildlife are at risk from polluted waterways.

Water pollution

The paper manufacturing industry uses more water per tonne of product than any other industry. Vast quantities of water and chemicals are used to bleach the pulp which need to be treated and cleaned after use.

⊕ The pulp and paper industry is the third largest industrial polluter to air, water and land in both Canada and the USA, and releases well over 100 million kg of toxic pollution each year. This paper mill in Brunswick, USA, sits on the Turtle River.

Mining

Mining for coal, metal ores and other precious metals or stones can damage the environment in several ways. Coal mining can leave huge holes in the ground and piles of unsightly **slag** that ruin the appearance of the landscape.

Gold mining is one of the dirtiest industries in the world. The production of just one gold ring generates 20 tonnes of mining waste. Open-pit gold mining uses a method where piles of crushed rock are soaked in a dangerous **cyanide** solution to extract the gold. If this solution is not carefully contained it can pollute the surrounding soil and water, killing many plants and animals and sometimes local people.

HOTSPOT:

Saying 'No' to dirty gold

Fourteen leading jewellery sellers from the UK and USA have said they will not buy gold from a proposed open-pit gold mine in Alaska. The proposed site is in an area of pristine wilderness, famous for its wild salmon.

Waste gases

Many industries and factories produce unwanted waste gases. A lot of these are poisonous or damaging to the environment.

Carbon dioxide

Burning **fossil fuels**, such as coal, oil and gas, releases carbon dioxide (CO_2) into the atmosphere. The level of this greenhouse gas has risen over the last 30 years and is thought to be responsible for the global warming of the world. Despite this, fossil fuels continue to be burned at an increasing rate because it is the cheapest way of producing electricity. Many countries have plans to reduce the amount of CO_2 they release by storing it underground using a method called **carbon capture and storage**. However, this process has not yet been fully tested, and nobody knows if it will work.

HOTSPOT:

Greenhouse gases in greenhouses!

Sometimes CO_2 can be recycled. At a sugar beet factory in the UK (right), waste CO_2 from the sugar production process is piped into nearby greenhouses to increase the **yield** of fruits and vegetables grown there.

Chlorofluorocarbons

Fridges used to contain chemicals called chlorofluorocarbons (CFCs). When an old fridge was scrapped, the CFCs were released into the atmosphere. These were found to be destroying the **ozone layer**. This layer of gas in the upper atmosphere is very important as it filters out **ultraviolet radiation** from the Sun. Most countries banned the use of CFCs in the 1990s and old fridges must now be taken to dedicated recycling centres to be dismantled. The ozone hole is now shrinking, although full recovery may not happen until about 2070.

This image shows the ozone hole (shown in pink) over Antarctica.

Methane

Methane is another greenhouse gas. It is thought that 18 per cent of the **greenhouse effect** is caused by methane. It is produced by living things in a variety of ways; by rice paddy fields, by swamps and wetlands, by grazing animals and, as we have seen, from rotting waste in landfill. We cannot do much about most of these sources, but the methane produced in landfill can be captured and used to generate electricity. The USA is currently spending $400 million building facilities at 60 landfills throughout the country to do this.

How can you help?

Help save the atmosphere by reducing the amount of electricity you use. Turn off lights and other electrical appliances when not in use.

A low-waste future

The United Nations estimates worldwide annual waste production to be at more than two billion tonnes, and increasing every year. It is clear that we need to impose stricter regulations on the creation and disposal of our waste.

Preventing waste

The way we deal with waste can be shown in a pyramid diagram. At present, most of our waste goes to landfill or is burned. This is the worst option. Further up the pyramid we reduce, reuse and recycle waste. The prevention of waste, the best option, is the least common, at the top. What we need to do is reverse the pyramid so that the largest volume of waste is prevented from occurring, and landfill and incineration options are greatly reduced.

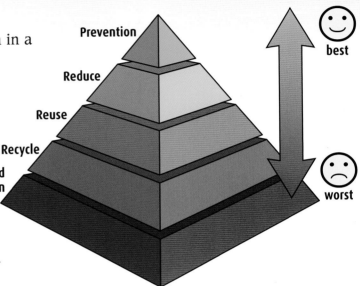

Prevention
Reduce
Reuse
Recycle
Landfill and incineration

best
worst

The Chinese use 45 billion pairs of disposable chopsticks a year, using the wood from 25 million trees! The Chinese government has now put a tax on disposable chopsticks and has urged restaurants not to use them. As a result over 400 restaurants in Beijing have promised to wash and reuse their chopsticks!

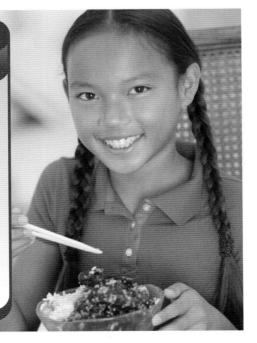

Dispose of disposables

There are many ways in which you can help prevent making waste. Have you noticed how many disposable products are available today? Disposable cameras, disposable razors, disposable nappies, disposable cups, plates and cutlery, batteries and, of course, plastic bags. Try to buy reusable things rather than disposable ones.

Working together to make less

Much work needs to be done by governments and manufacturing industries to reduce the volume of waste created by the world. But every one of us can take part in controlling our waste. Every battery you don't buy, every bag you reuse and every bottle you recycle is helping reduce the pressure of waste on our planet.

New York City spends around $1 million a day on moving rubbish. Here a tug-boat pushes a barge filled with crushed cars.

Glossary

Atmosphere
The layer of gases that surrounds the Earth.

Biodegradable
Something that will break down and rot naturally.

Biodigester
A machine that can process plant and animal waste to create electricity.

Carbon capture and storage
A method of storing carbon dioxide produced from power stations.

Compost
Decayed plant material that can be used to improve soil.

Coolant
A liquid, usually water, used to prevent overheating.

Cyanide
A very poisonous chemical.

Decompose
To break down through the action of bacteria and fungi.

Developing countries
Poorer countries where people have a low standard of living and low levels of industry.

Ecosystem
A community of living things together with their environment.

Evaporation
When something changes from a liquid into a gas.

Fertiliser
Chemicals that are put on the land to help the growth of crops.

Fossil fuels
Fuels such as coal, oil and natural gas that were formed underground millions of years ago.

Furnace
A very hot oven used to melt metals.

Global warming
A rise in the average temperature of the Earth which many people think is caused by an increase of greenhouse gases in the atmosphere.

Greenhouse effect
The warming of the Earth caused by a layer of insulating gases.

Greenhouse gases
Gases in the atmosphere, such as carbon dioxide or water vapour, that absorb heat that would otherwise escape into space.

Hazardous
Very dangerous.

Incinerate
To burn to ashes.

Landfill
A place where waste materials are buried in the ground.

Materials recovery facility
A place where waste materials are sorted.

Mineral ores
Rocks that contain metals.

Natural resources
Resources that are available naturally on the Earth, such as wood, oil, coal and water.

Ozone layer
The layer of ozone gas in the atmosphere.

Poisonous
Containing dangerous substances.

Radioactive
Capable of giving out energy in the form of powerful and harmful rays.

Raw materials
The basic material from which a product is made.

Recycle
The act of processing used materials for use in making new products.

Slag
A mixture of coal dust and rock waste that is left over after coal has been mined.

Smelting
Melting a mineral ore to get metal from it.

Ultraviolet radiation
Invisible rays from the Sun that can damage the skin and cause skin cancer.

Yield
The amount of crop produced.

Further information

Books

Food and Garden Waste (What happens when we recycle?)
Jillian Powell, Franklin Watts, 2009

Refuse Collection (How It Works)
James Nixon, Franklin Watts, 2009

Waste and Pollution (Sustaining our Environment)
Jill Laidlaw, Franklin Watts, 2009

Waste and Recycling (The Green Team)
Sally Hewitt, Franklin Watts, 2008

Dealing with Waste series
Sally Morgan, Franklin Watts, 2006

Websites

http://tonto.eia.doe.gov/kids/energy.cfm?page=environment_recycling-basics
Learn all about recycling from the Energy Information Administration.

www.ecy.wa.gov/programs/swfa/kidsPage
An interactive site that is designed to show the importance of waste reduction, recycling and solid waste management.

www.epa.gov/recyclecity/
Welcome to Recycle City. Find out how the people of Dumptown learned to reduce waste, save money and turn their town around.

www.go-recycle.org.uk/
All you need to know about recycling, reducing waste and sustainable lifestyles.

Index